# Cartooning for Kids!

# Fairy Tale Fun

By Dave Garbot

Publisher: Rebecca J. Razo

Art Director: Shelley Baugh

Project Editor: Janessa Osle

Senior Editor: Stephanie Meissner

Managing Editor: Karen Julian

Associate Editor: Jennifer Gaudet

Production Artists: Debbie Aiken, Amanda Tannen

Production Manager: Nicole Szawlowski

Production Coordinator: Lawrence Marquez


Illustrated and written by Dave Garbot

www.walterfoster.com

6 Orchard Road, Suite 100

Lake Forest, CA 92630

Printed in Shenzhen, China, January 2015

3 5 7 9 10 8 6 4 2

19207

# Table of Contents

# What You Will Need

crayons

eraser

colored
pencils

markers

pencil

# Getting Started

Fairy tales are always fun to read and listen to. However, since fairy tales are just stories, we have to use our imaginations or rely on the illustrations of an artist to help us follow along. In this book we'll do just that. We'll learn to draw many of the characters we've read about before, but with a silly twist to give them tons of personality. So grab your pencil, paper, and maybe a cookie too... Let's get started!

# Fantastical Features

Here are a few things you can use when drawing your characters. Maybe you'll want a different hairstyle, a beard, or fancy shoes! Come back to this section if you need some ideas!

## Hair

# Beards

# Mouths

# Feet

# The Magic Castle

Does your character need an accessory? Enter the magic castle, and choose an item that will complete your drawing and give it a silly twist!

11

# Famous Characters

In this section we'll draw characters that have been around for a long time. Stories have been written about them, and they've even been in the movies—they're famous! Everyone wants a picture with these stars, but since they can be hard to find in public, let's draw them instead!

# Robin Hood

Robin looks pretty happy. Can you give him different eyes?
How about a different mouth?

# Bo Peep

Bo Peep loves her sheep! Can you add a few more to her flock?

# Red Riding Hood

What if Red had a different color cape and hood? Then what would her name be? Start your drawing off with a simple circle, but don't worry if it's not perfectly round.

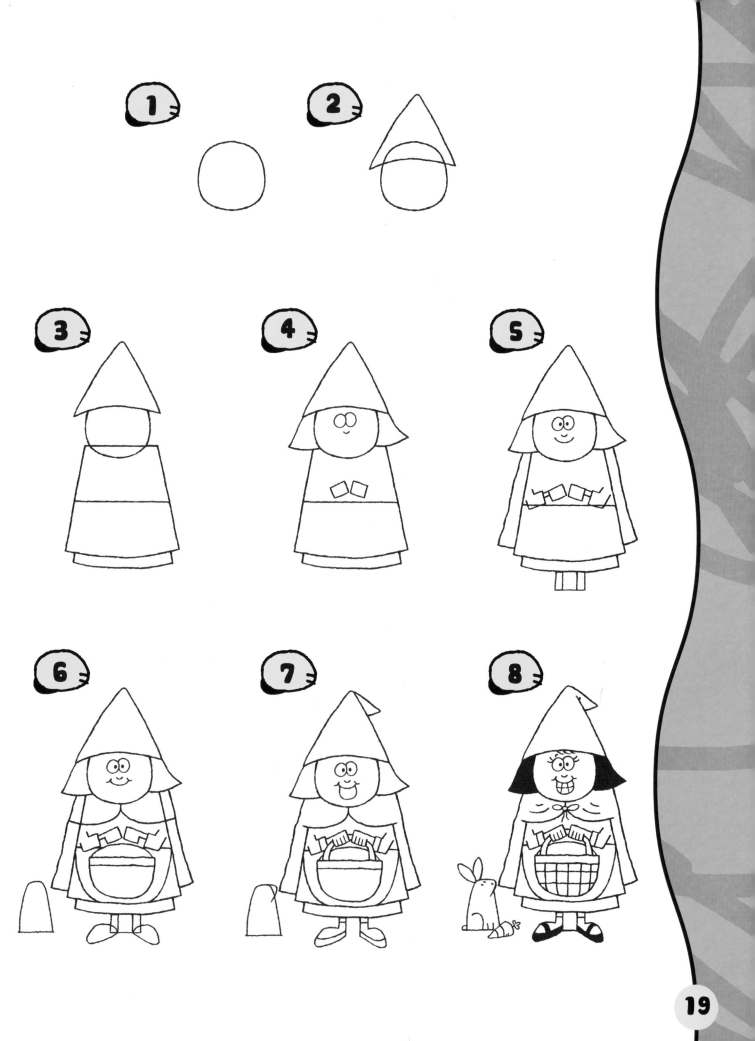

19

# Mother Goose

Can you give Mother Goose a different hat?

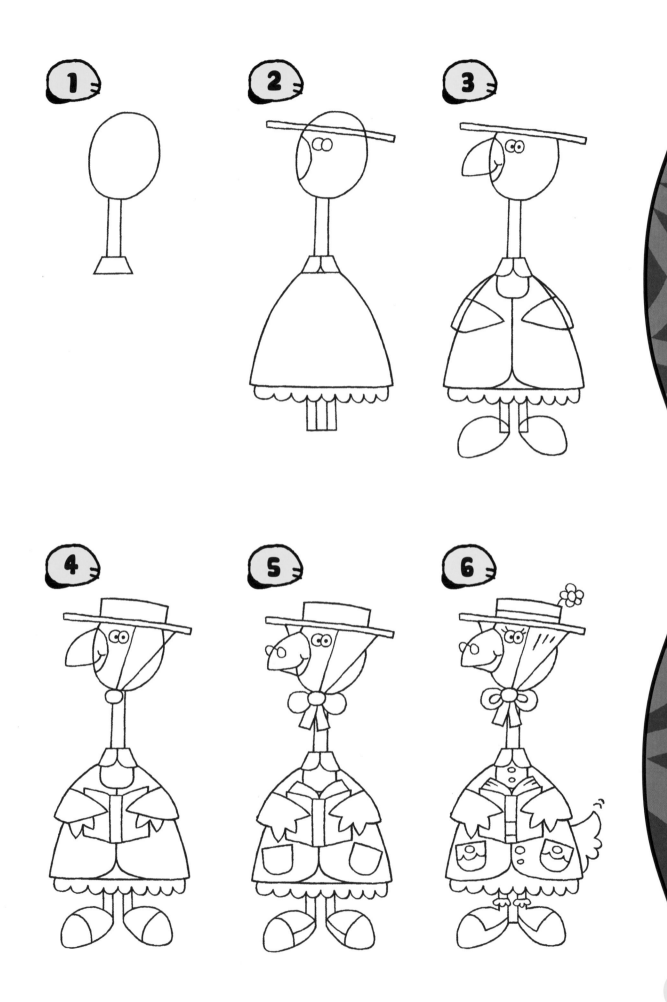

# The Three Little Pigs

We'll start with one pig, but you can draw his two little friends using the exact same steps! Color each pig a different color when you're done. Pig 1 can hold a piece of straw; Pig 2 can hold sticks; and Pig 3 can hold...what?

# Frog Prince

Can you add a pair of sunglasses to this groovy frog? Don't worry if your shapes aren't exact. Frogs come in all shapes and sizes!

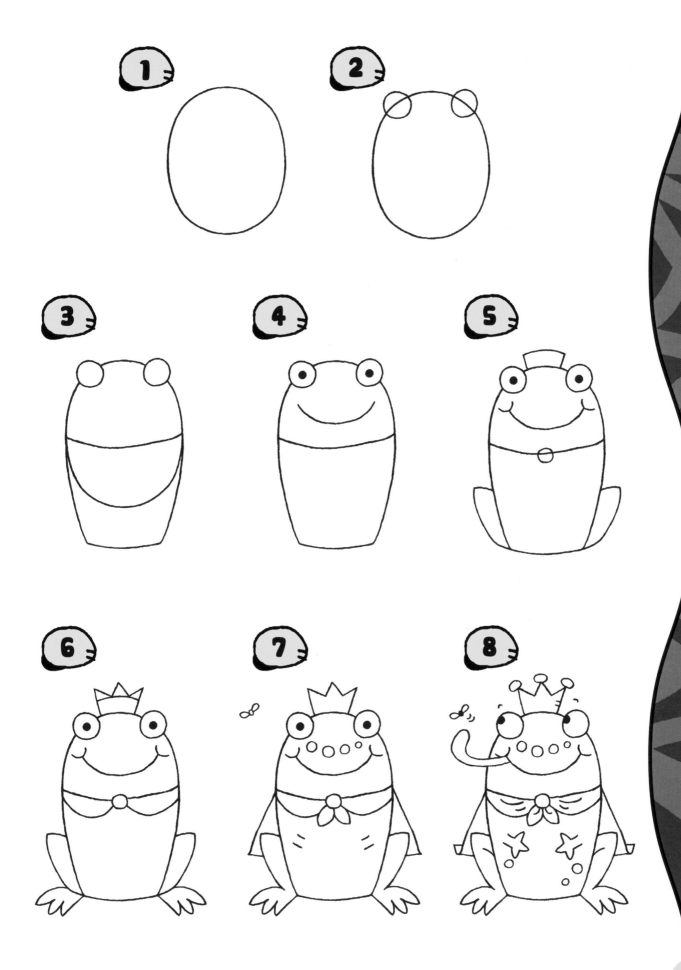

# Humpty Dumpty

If you make the wall shorter, Humpty might look less nervous!
Drawing an egg-like object is easier if you start with a middle line,
then draw one half at a time.

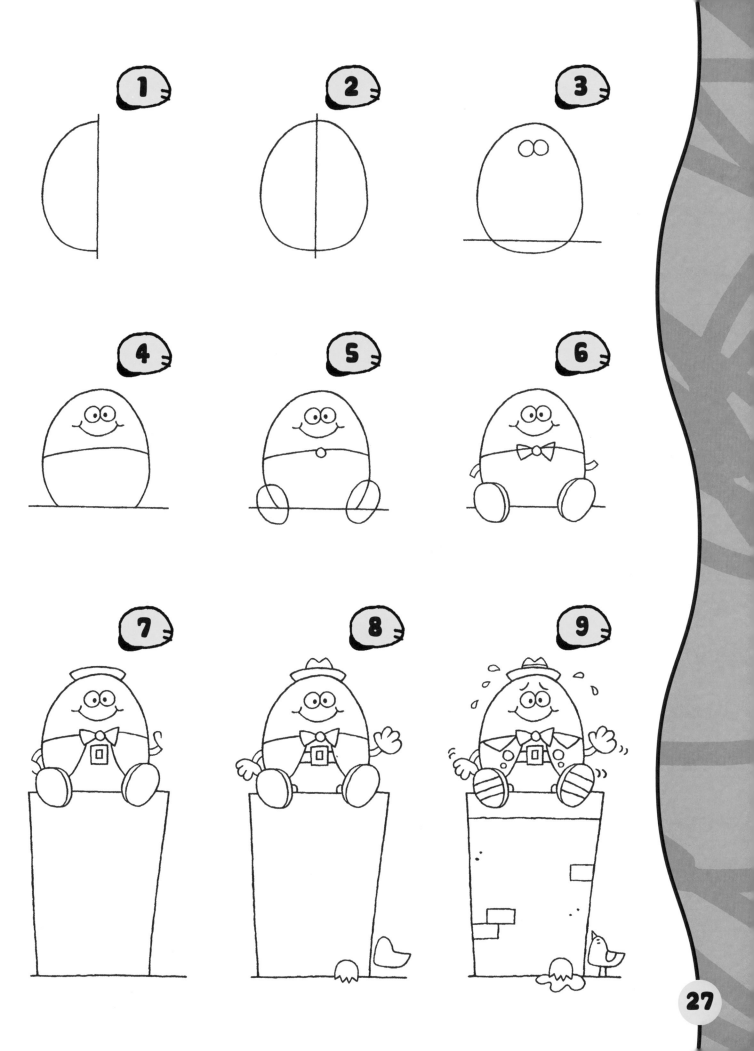

27

# The Three Bears

These bears are so cute. Looking back at some of the lessons we've already completed, do you think you could draw Goldilocks to join them? Maybe dress the bears in crazy costumes or give them new accessories!

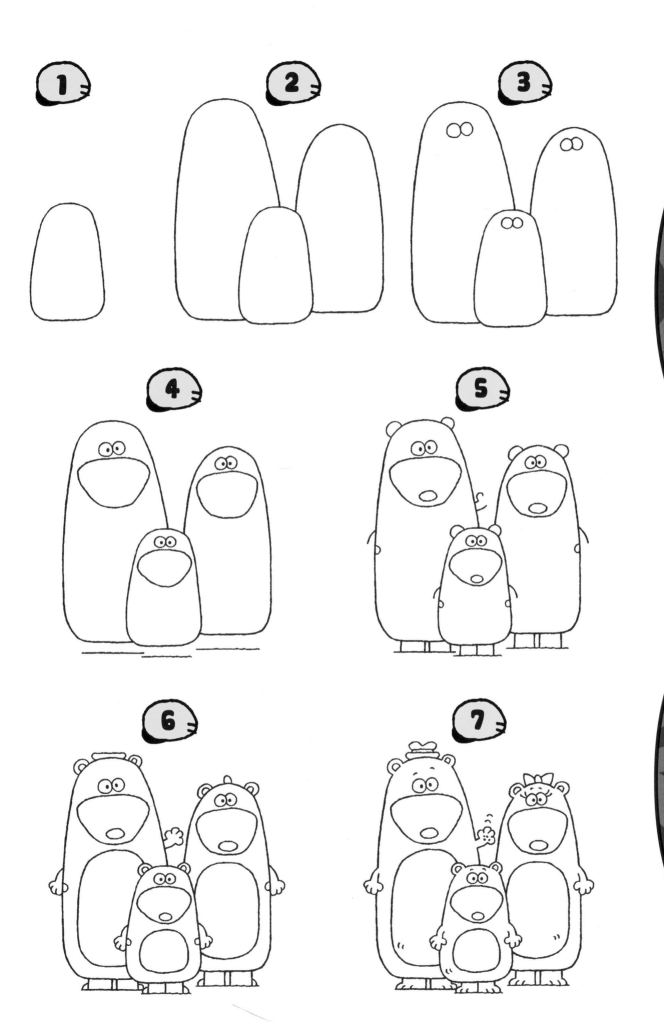

29

# Good Guys

The characters in this section are the good guys (and gals) of the fairy tale world. They are charming, brave, and they always live "happily ever after!" Have fun drawing them, because each one scores a perfect "10" with everyone they meet!

# Pretty Princess

Princesses usually have lots of dresses to wear. How would you change her dress to make it look different?

# Noble Knight

This knight is ready for anything. Can you draw him with his visor down to cover his face? Try changing his colors.

# Fairy Godmother

This fairy Godmother has two tiny feathered friends.
Can you add a few more to this group?

# King Kingston

The king is a happy guy. How would he look with sunglasses or a pair of sneakers?

39

# Queeny

The queen always wears a crown, but can you give her a different hat to wear?

41

# Prince Charming

Look! The prince has found a glass slipper. Can you change it to something else? How about a cheeseburger?

# Not-so-good Guys

The characters in this section are bad news. They usually appear in a story to cause trouble and give the good guys a hard time. They're just plain grumpy! Maybe you can make this group smile a little bit in your drawings!

# Witchy

How would Witchy look with a square top hat?
Try making her hair very straight or very curly!

# Pirate Paul

This pirate looks a little grumpy holding that sword. Can you draw him waving something else? How about a big fish or a feather?

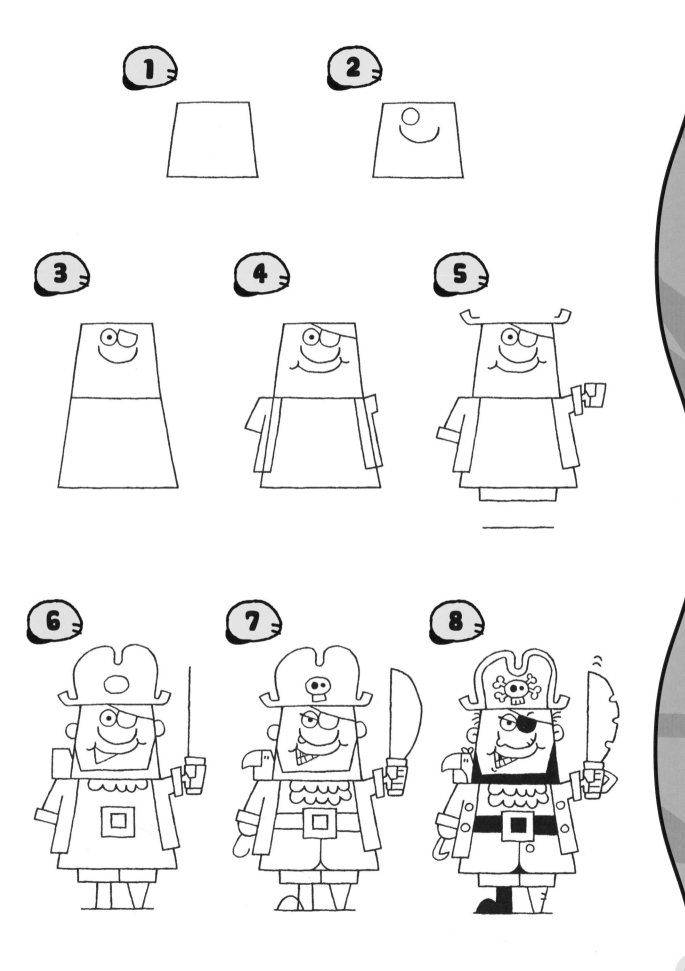

# Big Bad Wolf

If you changed his eyes, would this wolf still look mean?
Try drawing him without the line for his eyelids and see!

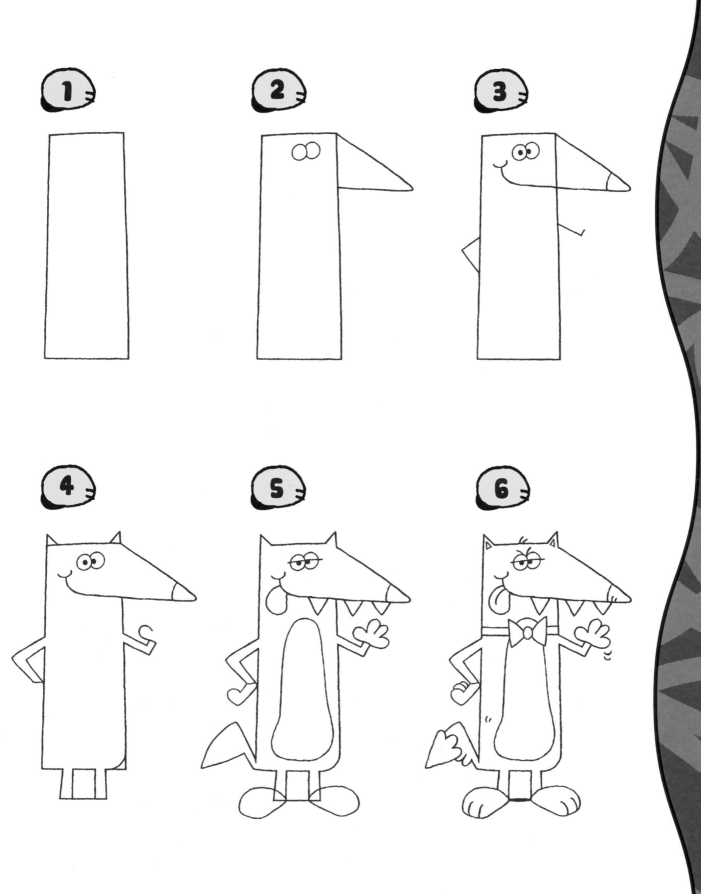

# Giant James

This grumpy giant has green skin, but you can change him to whatever color you like. How about blue? Do the sizes of the objects on the ground make your giant look tall? What would happen if you changed their sizes?

# Magical Creatures

You don't see the characters in this section every day. Sometimes in stories they have special powers! This group is a little quirky and different, but that makes them interesting and fun. You might even call them magical!

# Drake Dragon

Some fairy tale dragons like to fly. Try adding wings so this one can take off!

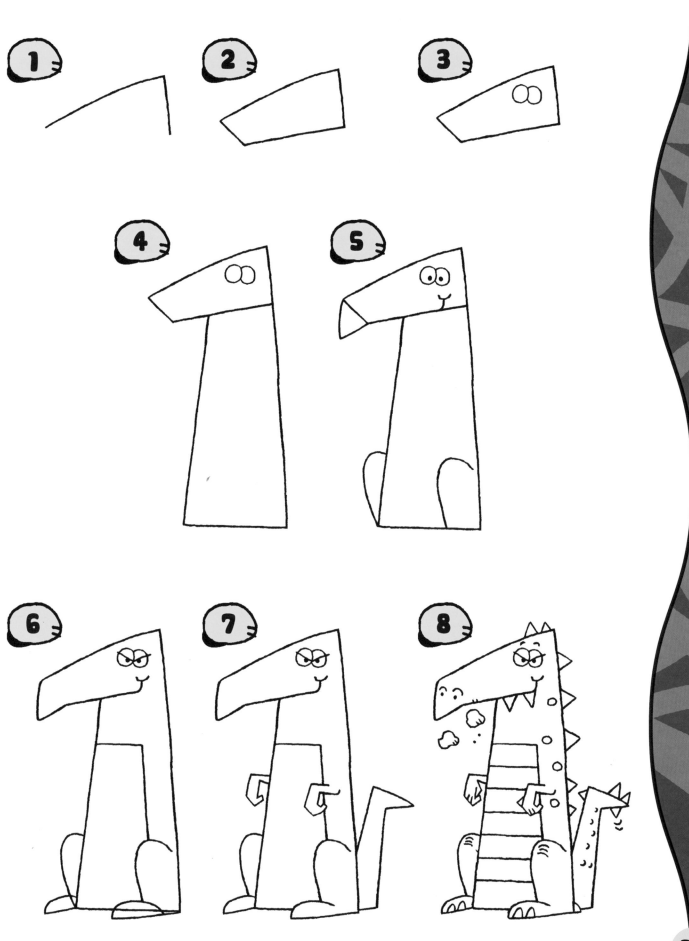

# Wiz

This wizard has some crazy swirls on his coat.
Can you change them to different kinds of shapes?
How about triangles or moons?

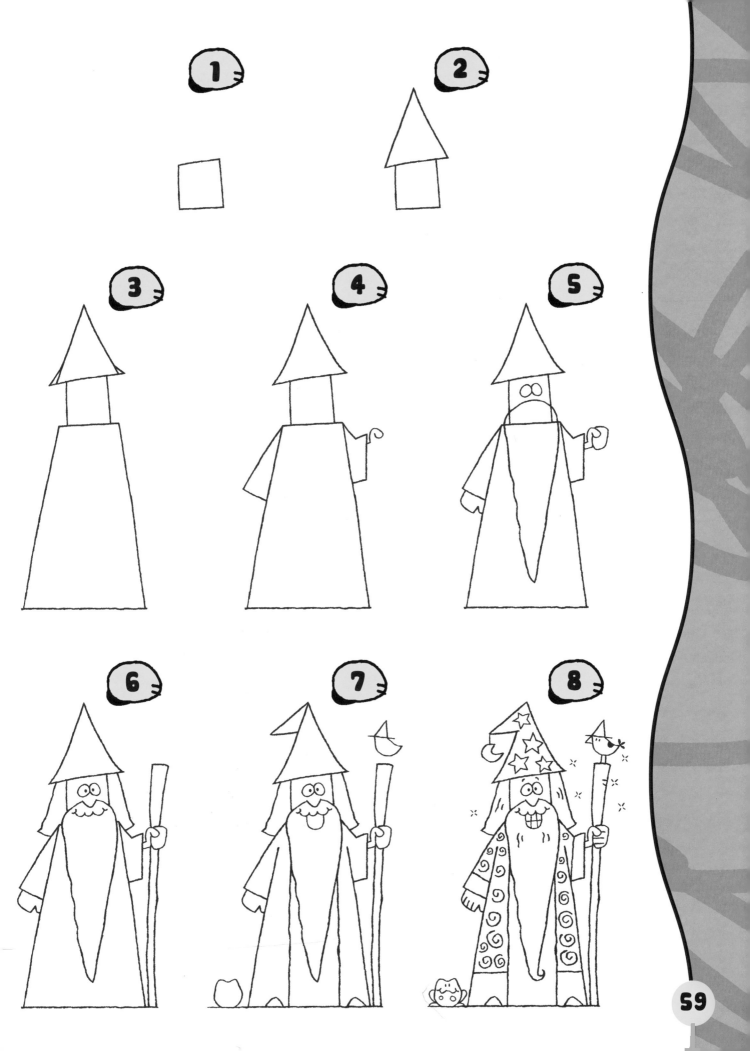

# Pinky Unicorn

Can you draw this pretty unicorn with its eyes open?

# Eddie Elf

Some stories have a whole bunch of crazy elves. Can you draw one, two, or maybe six more to join Eddie?

# About the Author

Dave Garbot is a professional illustrator and has been drawing for as long as he can remember. He is frequently called upon to create characters for children's books and other publications. Dave always has a sketchbook with him, and he gets many of his ideas from the things he observes every day, as well as from lots of colorful childhood memories. Although he admits that creating characters brings him personal enjoyment, making his audience smile, feel good, and maybe even giggle is what really makes his day.

Dave is from Portland, Oregon, and you can see more of his work at www.garbot.com.